www.osha.gov

I0483051

Occupational Safety and Health Act of 1970

"To assure safe and healthful working conditions for working men and women; by authorizing enforcement of the standards developed under the Act; by assisting and encouraging the States in their efforts to assure safe and healthful working conditions; by providing for research, information, education, and training in the field of occupational safety and health."

Firefighting Precautions at Facilities with Combustible Dust

Occupational Safety and Health Administration
U.S. Department of Labor

OSHA 3644-04 2013

TABLE OF CONTENTS

Introduction

Every year, a number of emergency responders are injured, and sometimes killed, during emergency operations in facilities where combustible dusts exist. In some cases, responders have inadequate information or training on the explosible[1] characteristics of combustible dust and/or the conditions present in the facility, which has increased the challenge of handling incidents safely and effectively.

When there is a delay or setback during an incident, the risk of injury rises for facility workers as well as for emergency responders. Everyone is safer when facility and emergency personnel share information and develop safe procedures to handle incidents involving combustible dusts. Owners, operators, and the community also benefit from reduced property damage when incidents are handled quickly and safely.

The primary purpose of this document is to protect emergency responders from harm by giving them a framework for gathering the necessary information prior to an emergency and converting it into safe operating procedures. In this document, emergency responders include firefighters, fire brigade members, hazardous materials teams, and others who might be called upon to respond when a fire or explosion occurs.

This document is not intended to provide specific strategies or tactics to be used during emergency responses. It does, however, discuss some tactics that should be considered. The information presented here and collected during pre-incident surveys should be used to train all emergency responders on how to properly handle incidents at facilities with combustible dusts.

The information presented in this publication is limited to the fire and explosion hazards of combustible dust. Facilities with combustible dust may have other hazards for emergency responders to consider, such as engulfment, electric shock, unguarded machinery and chemical toxins.

1. "Explosible" materials are capable of exploding; combustible dusts become capable of exploding when finely divided and dispersed as described in the next section. "Explosive" materials can explode as is; their main purpose is to function by explosion.

How does a combustible dust explosion occur?

Firefighters are well aware of the elements of the "fire triangle": fuel, heat, and oxygen (see figure 1). In this case, combustible dust is the fuel. Oxygen is usually available in the ambient air. In addition to, or in place of the oxygen, another chemical oxidizer may simulate oxygen in the combustion reaction. The following information discusses the additional elements needed for a flash fire or explosion to occur.

Figure 1. *Fire Triangle*

Just about any solid material that burns can be explosible when finely divided into a dust. For example, a piece of wood can become explosible when reduced to sawdust. Even materials that do not burn in larger pieces (such as aluminum or iron) can be explosible in dust form.

In school or training, you may have seen a demonstration involving a small container with flour or a similar material that was ignited, created a small fireball, and forced the lid of the container to lift. This can occur on a much larger scale in a building or confined space.

When combustible dust in the proper concentration is dispersed in a cloud, and then ignited, a flash fire occurs (see figure 2). This flash fire is like a larger version of the fireball in the classroom demonstration. It is much more dangerous to humans than an ordinary fire because it spreads too quickly to outrun. You may hear the term "deflagration"; this is a type of flash fire that is strong enough to cause damage to equipment or structures.

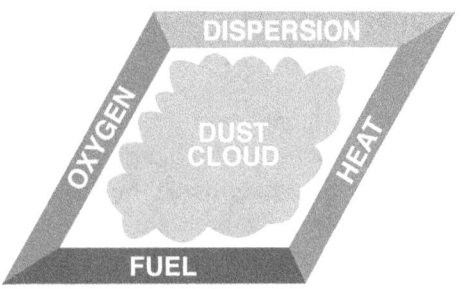

Figure 2. *Elements of a Flash Fire[2]*

When a flash fire is confined, the pressure that develops can cause an explosion, damaging or destroying the confining enclosure (see figure 3). This explosion is a larger version of the lifting lid in the classroom demonstration above. The confining enclosure could be processing equipment, a conveyor, a dust collector, a room, or an entire building. The flying shrapnel, blast wave and collapsing structural members resulting from the explosion can injure or kill individuals over a large area.

Figure 3. *Explosion Pentagon*

The blast wave can also disperse accumulated combustible dust in work or storage areas, fueling one or more subsequent explosions. These secondary explosions are often more destructive than the initial incident due to the large quantities of dust dispersed. Secondary explosions can continue to ignite in sequence, cascading throughout a facility.

2. This four-sided representation of flash fire elements should not be confused with a fire tetrahedron, which adds an element (chemical chain reaction) to the fire triangle to explain how certain agents extinguish a fire.

What do previous incidents illustrate?

Firefighting operations can inadvertently increase the chance of a combustible dust explosion if they:

- Use tactics that cause dust clouds to form or reach the explosible range.
- Use tactics that introduce air, creating an explosible atmosphere.
- Apply incorrect or incompatible extinguishing agents.
- Use equipment or tools that can become an ignition source.

The examples below illustrate these general principles in specific incidents. In some examples, combustible dust fueled the entire event; in others, combustible dust may have contributed to it. In most cases, the initial ignition sequence is unknown or unreported.

- **South Dakota, 2011: two firefighters killed.** According to a National Institute for Occupational Safety and Health (NIOSH) report, a fire occurred in a coal bin that fed a boiler. Firefighters brought it under control at first, but it flared up again. Two firefighters then climbed onto the roof and directed a water hose stream through a hatch. An explosion killed both of them (see figure 4). The explosion may have involved combustible dust, flammable gases, steam, or a combination of these factors.

Photo: NIOSH

Figure 4. *Coal bin explosion*

Wisconsin, 2010: one firefighter killed and eight injured. According to a NIOSH report, foundry workers improperly placed a barrel of hot slag in a recycling dumpster with aluminum shavings, and a fire resulted. The local fire department had not conducted a proper pre-incident survey of the facility and was unaware of the incompatibility of water and burning metals. They attacked the fire with water first, and then foam. Despite making no progress toward extinguishing the fire, as well as visual warnings such as bluish-green flames, the firefighters continued to attack the fire at close range. An explosion killed one of them and injured eight others (see figure 5).

Figure 5. Dumpster explosion

Oregon, 2010: one firefighter injured. News reports indicated that a fire occurred in sawdust waste on a conveyor at a forest products plant. A spark sensor and interlock operated properly and shut down the conveyor. When an access door was opened, the inrush of air triggered an explosion that injured a firefighter.

Unknown location, 2004: two firefighters injured. A National Fire Protection Association (NFPA) report on firefighter injuries described a smoldering fire in ductwork at a furniture manufacturing company. Plant personnel told the fire department that the associated dust collector had been shut down, but it had not. Two firefighters on an aerial lift were injured when they gained access to the duct and an inrush of air caused an explosion.

Maryland, 2005: four firefighters injured. A fire department responded to light smoke coming from a sawdust hopper at a boat manufacturing plant. Two firefighters opened an access door and directed a straight stream of water onto the burning sawdust. A dust cloud discharged from the door, ignited immediately, and injured both firefighters (see figure 6 and cover). A second team of firefighters, unable to confer with the injured firefighters, repeated the attack using the same tactics. The same sequence of events recurred and they were also injured.

Figure 6. Sawdust hopper flash fire

Ohio, 2003: two firefighters killed, eight injured. According to a NIOSH report, several fire departments were fighting a fire at a lumber company in an oxygen-limiting silo that was filled with wood chips. Firefighters were directing water streams through openings at the base and the top of the silo when there was an explosion. A firefighter on top of the silo and another on an aerial platform were killed (see figure 7). The report cited improper tactics for oxygen-limiting silos as a factor in the outcome.

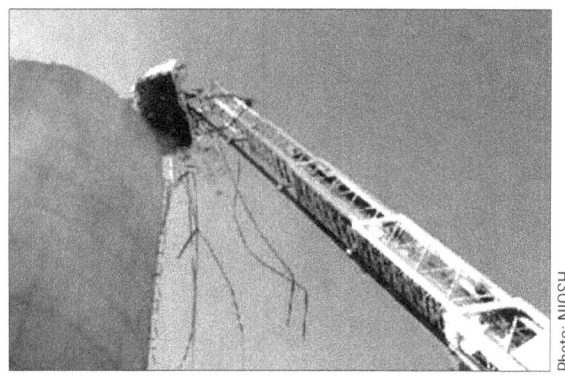

Figure 7. Wood chip silo explosion

What preparations can be made prior to a response?

Pre-incident survey

Many emergency response agencies routinely perform pre-incident surveys at facilities with special hazards. This allows responders, regardless of the size of the jurisdiction, to learn about the hazards, proper methods to handle emergencies, and the features in place to assist them (for example, water supplies, suppression systems, confined spaces, egress points). Emergency responders should treat combustible dust as a special hazard. This document is intended to provide guidance on supplementing the routine pre-incident survey to include combustible dust hazards.

A facility may produce, collect, or store dusts and/or dust-producing materials as its main operation or as an incidental matter. In either case, emergency responders need to know about combustible dust hazards in advance. This helps them plan appropriate actions and avoid creating additional hazards to themselves or occupants. All locations where combustible dust is used (including process or conveying equipment), produced (for example, cutting or grinding equipment), or stored (including all vessels, containers, or collectors) should be identified in the survey (see figure 8).

Facilities can have a variety of materials, operations, and procedures. Appendices A through D at pages 14–23 contain *general* information about these aspects of operations. During the pre-incident survey, it is important to collect *facility-specific* information on all of these aspects. This will make it possible to tailor emergency operations to a particular facility.

The pre-incident survey team should walk through the entire facility and consider each process, possibly by functional area, to identify the operations or components that generate, or could generate, enough dust to create a flash fire or explosion hazard. The team should consider all normal and potential abnormal (upset) conditions to ensure that the pre-incident survey is as comprehensive as possible. Consider organizing the information by facility areas or process areas for clarity.

Combustible dust can accumulate on any upward-facing surface. Fine dusts can even cling to vertical surfaces (see figure 9). A large amount of combustible dust often accumulates overhead, on structural components or other surfaces where it is hard to notice or clean. Historically, these dust accumulations are associated with cascading secondary explosions that lead to major or total facility loss. The team must consider all spaces—both exposed and hidden and at any elevation—in the pre-incident survey.

Figure 8. Sawdust spilled from equipment

Figure 9. Sawdust clinging to horizontal and vertical surfaces

Other sources of information are the jurisdiction's building construction and fire code officials.

In many cases the fire official is within the fire department, but this is not always the case. State and local fire codes often require permits for hazardous materials. In some cases, operational permits may be specifically required for combustible dust-producing operations. Such permits can serve as triggers for the pre-incident survey and can also contain specific facility information.

The pre-incident survey should cover metal dusts carefully. Note the presence of water-reactive metals and metal dusts. The importance of this is discussed in the section below on extinguishing agent selection.

The pre-incident survey forms the basis of how emergency responders plan for and handle incidents. Responders and facility representatives should discuss compatible extinguishing agents and appropriate attack methods during the survey. The section below regarding operational planning covers considerations and precautions in more detail.

Trade secrets

A company may be reluctant to disclose certain facts about a facility to the survey team, for fear of revealing trade secrets. But employers and firefighters must understand that the more specific the information that is shared, the more comprehensive and valuable the pre-incident survey will be. Explaining the negative effects of an incomplete or inadequate survey to the facility managers can help them realize the importance of disclosing as much relevant information as possible. When trade secrets are divulged to emergency responders, they must understand the importance of keeping this information secure.

Safety Data Sheets

Emergency responders should always consult Safety Data Sheets (SDSs) for all materials present. They can be a good source of basic information that should be supplemented by information specific to the facility's processes and operations. SDSs were previously called Material Safety Data Sheets (MSDSs).

Responders should also understand the limitations of SDSs. For some materials, SDSs may be unavailable because of the emergency or response situation, or may not be comprehensive because SDSs do not account for unanticipated uses and unforeseen emergencies. Chemical manufacturers are required to indicate hazards under normal conditions or in foreseeable emergencies (including those anticipated during downstream processing). Responders should heed warnings on any SDS, but should also consider possible explosion hazards even when SDSs do not mention them.

Hybrid mixtures

Emergency responders should be aware of the potential for hybrid mixtures. These are mixtures of flammable gas or vapor and combustible dust suspended in air. Hybrid mixtures can be explosible below either the lower flammable limit for the gas/vapor or the minimum explosible concentration for the dust.

Processes can involve hybrid mixtures routinely or during abnormal conditions. Potential flammable gas and vapor sources include fuel pipes to heating equipment, fuel tanks on material-handling equipment, and flammable liquid containers. Flammable gas can also be produced when a fire's combustion by-products become mixed with suspended dust. For example, carbon monoxide is a product of incomplete combustion and is a toxic, flammable gas often produced in dangerous amounts by smoldering fires. Any of these flammable gases or vapors can form hybrid mixtures with combustible dust.

Hybrid mixtures often migrate and become trapped by building features or equipment. Responders should be aware of ceiling height and potential trap areas.

Protection systems

Equipment and buildings with known combustible dust hazards should be equipped with devices or systems to prevent an explosion, minimize its propagation, or limit the damage it causes. Examples include relief vents or abort gates that direct damaging pressure or burning material out of a confined area (see figure 10) and isolation devices that prevent damaging pressure or fire from extending to another piece of equipment. Facilities can use special high-speed detection and suppression systems as well as oxygen-reduction systems. The team should note all these devices and systems in the pre-incident survey; this will let emergency responders support the systems or avoid making them ineffective during an incident.

Figure 10. Abort gate in duct

Both fire and explosion hazards of combustible dusts are often present in a facility. Ordinary fire suppression systems can be installed to address fire hazards. When such systems are provided in areas with explosion hazards (such as a silo or dust collector), they will only be effective for a fire and not for an explosion. These situations should be noted during the pre-incident survey. Precautions are discussed in greater detail in the section below on Fire Safety Systems section on page 10.

Facility liaison

The facility's staff is usually the best resource on the nature and extent of hazardous dust conditions present. To get a complete and accurate accounting of the materials, processes, and potential hazards, those performing the pre-incident survey will often need to discuss these issues with multiple members of the facility's organization. Staff from the safety, operations, maintenance, production, and facility engineering departments can provide valuable input, as can employee representatives.

Facilities should designate a specific person responsible for updating the emergency responders on any changes that affect the hazards at the facility. Ideally, this representative, and one or more alternates, will also be available as emergency contacts. An on-site liaison should report to the incident commander at the start of an emergency operation.

Emergency responders should obtain contact information for all facility emergency contacts, storing this information in a way that facilitates rapid communication during an incident. Facilities should ensure that any changes in representatives or their contact information are communicated to response agencies.

It is also a good idea for emergency responders and facility personnel to train together regularly. Knowing each other and the facility will promote a more efficient and effective response if an incident occurs.

Equipment compatibility

Finally, firefighters should ensure that on-site firefighting equipment is compatible with their equipment. For example, they should check whether the facility's fire hydrants, standpipe systems, and fire department inlet connections have the same hose threads as those used by the fire department. If the equipment is not compatible, it is best for the facility's equipment to be changed to match the fire department's. Alternatively, or as an interim measure, the facility can use adapters—either stored at the facility or carried by the fire department.

How should this preparation affect the operational plan?

Fire departments and fire brigades should use the information from the pre-incident survey to develop a draft Incident Action Plan (IAP). An IAP is a component of the National Incident Management System plan that is used throughout the United States to mitigate situations necessitating an emergency response. The IAP is more specific than the general Standard Operating Plans (SOPs) and Standard Operating Guidelines (SOGs) that the fire service uses to streamline typical emergency operations. Facility representatives that help conduct the pre-incident survey can often provide helpful input in the IAP development.

The draft IAP should consider all the precautions discussed in the next section. It should also take into account the information collected during the pre-incident survey described in the previous section, including specific materials, processes, equipment and protection systems.

During an emergency response to a facility (see figure 11), the fire service and other responders can implement the IAP. SOPs or SOGs guide their general operations, as modified by the facility-specific IAP. If an incident involves unexpected conditions, the IAP should be modified with the help of the information in the pre-incident survey and facility personnel. Together, planning and operational flexibility keep responders safe.

Figure 11. A fire department at the scene of a building fire

Responders should decide the best way to record both the pre-incident survey information and the IAP to enable ready access during an incident. It is crucial that this method allow these documents to be available even if memories fade and personnel changes. Whether the storage mode is written or electronic, expedited retrieval is essential.

All responders who might be called to a facility should be able to access the pre-incident survey information and the IAP. This likely means sharing the information with all fire stations expected to respond, whether within the same department or not. Fire departments (of all sizes) often have arrangements with other nearby departments to provide assistance through "mutual aid" agreements.

What precautions can be taken during a response?

Fire Attack Mode

One of the first decisions during an emergency incident is whether to attack the fire offensively (see figure 12) or to contain it defensively; a rapid risk assessment must be conducted with the information available. This becomes more important during responses that involve materials subject to flash fires or explosions (including combustible dusts) because of the speed of the combustion and the large potential exposure areas.

Figure 12. Firefighters performing an interior (offensive) fire attack

One main consideration in the decision regarding attack mode is the structural stability of the building or equipment involved. By definition, an explosion causes structural damage to the confining enclosure. However, even a flash fire can weaken structural components due to the intense heat involved. Responders may arrive to find that a flash fire has occurred but not propagated; they should not assume that the building or vessel is structurally sound simply because the fire is extinguished.

The attack posture can also be changed during an incident. The appearance of a persistent dust cloud or the discovery of significant accumulations of combustible dust should trigger the same considerations and precautions as any other material that could explode.

The explosibility of a dust cloud is difficult, if not impossible, to measure during an incident. Meters are available to measure for explosible levels of flammable gases and vapors, but none are currently available for combustible dusts. One rule of thumb: if the dust cloud totally obscures a light source at a distance of 6 to 9 feet, treat it as if it is in the explosible range, and consider evacuating the area.

A hybrid mixture's explosion limit is very difficult to predict precisely because there are infinite combinations of gas and dust concentrations, and their relative amounts are likely not uniform throughout a dust cloud. Emergency responders commonly use flammable gas and vapor meters (often two to validate results), but there is no test equipment that will determine if a hybrid mixture has reached explosion limits.

Dusts can also interfere with meters for flammable gases and vapors by depositing residue on sensors. Filtering material to remove the dust may protect the sensors, but the meters should be checked frequently for loss of sample flow. Some meters will provide an alarm upon reduction or loss of this flow. Responders must remember that the reading on the meter is only for the flammable gas and vapor component; it does not include the hazard contribution from the dust. A mixture of flammable gas or vapor and combustible dust can be more energetic than either individual component.

Extinguishing Agent Selection

The main precaution in choosing extinguishing agents is to use only agents that are compatible with the materials present—both those burning and those just nearby. For example, using water or any water-based agents (such as foam) on any burning combustible metals (such as magnesium, aluminum, and titanium) can cause an explosible reaction. Alkali metals (such as sodium and potassium) will react violently with water even if they are not burning. Wetted alkali metals may generate hydrogen gas, and this gas may not register on a traditional 4-gas meter.

The type and quantity of extinguishing agent must also be able to extinguish the materials involved in a fire. Examples include class C agents for live electrical equipment and class D agents for combustible metals (see figure 13).

Photo: M. Chibbaro

Figure 13*. Class D fire extinguisher*

If materials present are all class A, consider the use of wetting agents. These reduce the surface tension of the water. Wetting agents help the water penetrate and extinguish deep-seated fires, particularly those in densely-packed material.

A reference chart for extinguishing agents suitable for various combustible metals is contained in the National Fire Protection Association (NFPA) book *Guide to Combustible Dusts* or its standard 484, *Standard for Combustible Metals*. The chart also indicates which agent is the preferred one for each metal.

Complicating extinguishing agent selection is the potential for multiple fuels to be involved in a fire, with no single extinguishing agent available rated to extinguish all of them. If the fuels cannot be separated, it will likely be necessary to take a defensive attack posture and allow the fire to burn out on its own.

Reactivity between extinguishing agents and chemicals is a further concern. Reference information is available on the *Chemical Reactivity Worksheet* from the National Oceanic and Atmospheric Administration or in NFPA's book, *Fire Protection Guide to Hazardous Materials*.

Fire Extinguisher Use

Just as selecting an appropriate extinguishing agent is important, properly applying the agent is crucial to a successful outcome. When using extinguishers, responders must avoid dispersing combustible dusts into the air. Typically, extinguishers are aimed directly at the base of the flames. To avoid dust clouds, responders should use the extinguisher from as far away as possible and apply the agent as gently as possible. Pressurized class D extinguishers are designed for gentle application, but care must still be exercised. Class D extinguishing agents can also be stored in containers and applied with a scoop or shovel.

Fire extinguishers are often available at facilities for use on specific hazardous materials, including combustible dust. If so, emergency responders should plan to use these existing extinguishers.

Hose Stream Use

The main considerations with hose stream operation are to avoid creating combustible dust clouds or introducing more air. In particular, the use of solid streams can disperse dust into the air. The use of wide-pattern (or "fog") streams at pressures typically used for firefighting can move large quantities of air, which is why firefighters often use such streams to "hydraulically ventilate" spaces.

The best way to apply water is in a medium to wide-pattern, as gently as possible (see figure 14). Responders should use a low nozzle pressure and loft the stream onto the burning material from as far away as the stream will reach.

Photo: M. Chibbaro

Figure 14. *Low pressure, medium fog hose stream*

Solid streams can be used from a safe distance where farther reach is necessary. If still in an area subject to the effects of an explosion (e.g., fireball, pressure wave, shrapnel), the nozzle should be set up with covering hose streams and then left operating unmanned.

Responders may consider using solid streams to overhaul piles of fully wetted material. However, determining if the pile is wet all the way through can be difficult or impossible. If dry material remains inside the pile or on its bottom, it could be dispersed by the hose stream.

Another tool that may be effective in certain circumstances is a piercing nozzle. These are designed to penetrate an enclosure, making it possible to apply water without entering or even opening the enclosure. Such nozzles are commonly used on coal bunker fires. The penetration point, spray pattern, and nozzle pressure must still be considered to minimize dust dispersal within the enclosure. Responders should not get a false sense of security just because personnel are outside the enclosure; they should consider if they can still be affected by an explosion.

In addition to extinguishment, water from hose lines can be used to render dust accumulations safe. Gently wetting piles of dust will make it too heavy to disperse into a cloud. Because a large amount of water can be trapped within the piles rather than run off, structural stability could become a problem—but here, again, planning can help.

Some class A materials, such as coal, are known to heat up when wetted. Do not use water as a preventive measure on such fuels.

Overall, give preference to using medium- to wide-spray patterns rather than solid streams. Use as low a pressure as possible to provide the stream reach necessary.

Fire Safety Systems

Fire protection systems designed for fires will likely not protect against flash fires or explosions. For example, a sprinkler system designed to control fires is typically designed for sprinklers to open over an area expected to be involved in a fire. A flash fire could easily activate a far greater number of sprinkler heads than the design considered, resulting in inadequate water pressure and ineffective fire control. An explosion could damage a significant portion of the system, also rendering it ineffective. This can even occur where an incident occurs in outside equipment arranged to recirculate exhaust back into an interior space and an abort mechanism is not provided. Responders should therefore have a good understanding of the capabilities and limitations of such systems.

Responders might also encounter more specialized fixed systems for fire and explosion prevention, detection, protection, or suppression. A safe and successful outcome requires a clear understanding of these specialized (and often unique) systems before interacting with them.

Some systems have hazards inherent in their operation. One example is explosion suppression systems that must activate at speeds high enough to stop explosions in progress; these systems likely employ explosive actuators. Some systems apply agents at a concentration unsafe for humans without proper respiratory protection. Other systems need an enclosure to contain the extinguishing agent; ventilating or accessing such an enclosure prematurely can negate its effectiveness.

Responders should also be aware of inerting systems that use an agent such as nitrogen or carbon dioxide to reduce the oxygen available and thus prevent a fire or explosion. Self-contained breathing apparatus is necessary in such an environment. Ventilation and access activities can reduce the effectiveness of such systems and introduce oxygen to form an explosive atmosphere. In a few rare situations, inerting can be a useful form of suppression if the agent and a safe delivery system are available.

There have been reports of two issues associated with dry-pipe or deluge sprinkler systems:

1. As they fill with water, such system's pipes can shake. This can dislodge combustible dust that has accumulated on them, contributing to the fire.

2. Air discharged from the system (before water begins to discharge) can both disperse dusts accumulated nearby and introduce more air in the immediate vicinity of the fire.

Finally, emergency responders should coordinate with facility personnel before shutting down any protection or prevention system.

Access

Gaining access to the interior of process equipment, dust collection equipment, conveying equipment, or storage elements (see Appendices A through D) can be dangerous due to the possibility of dislodging dust or allowing dust to fall out, which could create an immediate dust explosion hazard. Such access can also introduce additional air flow to support a fire or explosion. It is important, therefore, to thoroughly understand the ramifications of gaining access before doing so, and to consider the proper timing of ventilation and power shutdown.

A thermal imaging camera can be a valuable tool in this situation. It can provide information about where hidden burning materials are located, and thereby assist in the decision regarding whether or when to gain access.

If opening an access panel (see figure 15) is necessary, consider protecting nearby firefighters with a covering hose stream. Responders should work with the facility's liaison or emergency contacts to find the safest access procedure—the one that will contain dust clouds or keep them from forming.

Figure 15. *Access panel, walkway, and ladder on equipment*

Dust collection systems (see Appendix A) typically use negative pressure; thereby collecting dust with exhaust hoods, sweeps, extraction points, and ducts. Rupturing or opening most ductwork for negative pressure systems while operating should not release much dust, but will likely reduce the air velocity and cause dust to accumulate within ducts. Every system is different, however, and the planning activities should consider the specific characteristics of the system in question. Note that dust collection baghouses and cyclones are especially likely to have significant accumulations of combustible dust, so emergency response activities involving these components should be well thought out.

Pneumatic conveying systems—common in many industries—are typically positive pressure systems used to transport materials between points in a process. These systems move solid materials, including collected dust, by suspending the material in high-velocity air. For example, combustible sugar and flour are often transported this way.

If a pneumatic conveying pipe, tube, duct, or piece of equipment is opened or has a structural failure while solid materials are moving, an explosible dust cloud could develop quickly outside the system. Emergency responders should be aware of this in case such a failure occurs during the incident and the pneumatic conveyance system is still operational.

Ventilation

Firefighters regularly use ventilation as a tactic to remove heat and smoke during fire attack and overhaul. When combustible dust is involved, ventilation—particularly at the wrong time—can have catastrophic consequences.

Ventilating specific pieces of equipment (e.g., for processing, conveying, or dust collection) can have the same consequences as accessing them (see the previous section). Responders should carefully consider if ventilation is an appropriate tactic and, if so, they should time it to minimize the flash fire or explosion hazard. It may be appropriate to ventilate only after complete wetting of surfaces and dust accumulations.

Using fans (either negative or positive pressure) to ventilate rooms or buildings can create sufficiently high air velocities to dislodge dust and suspend it in a cloud. Fans can also introduce more air into a space, which can create or worsen an explosible situation. Gas-powered positive pressure fans can introduce additional carbon monoxide into a facility during operation.

Responders may also encounter explosion vents installed on buildings or equipment. These devices are meant to relieve the pressure caused by a flash fire or explosion—preferably to a safe location. In some cases, they are not installed properly and are directed to inside work areas. Whether the vents are directed properly or not, responders should know their location to avoid being in the path of a venting flash fire or explosion.

Power Shutdown

Firefighters commonly shut down sources of power early in the operation. Here again, responders must ensure that power shutdown is the appropriate course of action, or at least consider the proper timing of the shutdown, and must understand the full implications of power shutdown before taking such actions. Coordination with plant personnel is essential—both to safely de-energize equipment, and to properly lockout/tagout equipment to prevent re-energizing during emergency operations.

Different courses of action may be appropriate for process systems, conveying systems, dust collection systems, and overall building power. For example, some dust collection systems need power to keep dust contained; shutting down power can create a dust cloud where none existed. Main power shutdown may disable fire detection and protection systems unless they are supplied by a secondary or emergency power source such as a generator.

Responders must take care when shutting down a pneumatic conveying system, especially if ignition sources are present. They must also evaluate the trade-offs associated with shutting down the system versus stopping the introduction of the material and allowing the system to purge itself. It may be prudent to allow conveying systems to run so that they can remove burning material from dryers or dust collectors. Consider the impact of either choice on the process equipment; it should not create further hazards.

Changes to the operating status of processing equipment can introduce abnormal (upset) conditions that could lead to fires, flash fires, or explosions. For example, shutting down power to a process stream without running out the product could trap that product in a dryer, where it might overheat and ignite. Responders should plan for possible scenarios and corresponding strategies for shutting down processes and the main power supply. They should also identify conditions under which power or process streams can safely be shut down.

Emergency responders should understand the proper rating of electrical equipment for dust explosion hazards. They may be familiar with Class I-rated equipment for flammable gases and vapors. The rating necessary to prevent ignition of combustible dust clouds is Class II. Responders should be sure to look for the proper rating for the corresponding hazard and remember that multiple ratings are necessary for multiple hazards. Finally, regardless of the planning done and precautions taken, emergency responders should operate under the assumption that ignition sources are always present.

Tool and Equipment Use

Emergency responders might carry tools that are not appropriate for use near combustible dust hazards. The wrong tool can introduce ignition sources. These might include portable fuel-fired tools, non-classified electrical equipment, or spark-producing hand tools. Non-sparking tools such as scoop shovels or natural-bristle brooms may be appropriate for certain situations or materials; if so, they are often available at the facility.

Emergency responders may be called upon to clean up combustible dust, especially during overhaul operations. Do so with care and with the advice of facility representatives. Any portable vacuum equipment used to remove combustible dust must be rated for dust explosion hazards (Class II hazardous areas) so that they do not present an ignition source. Vacuum hoses must be conductive or grounded to prevent static electricity buildup and discharge.

Where can I find additional information?

OSHA

- Combustible Dust Safety and Health Topics page: www.osha.gov/dsg/combustibledust/index.html
- Safety and Health Information Bulletin: www.osha.gov/dts/shib/shib073105.html
- Combustible Dust Explosions Fact Sheet: www.osha.gov/OshDoc/data_General_Facts/OSHAcombustibledust.pdf
- Combustible Dust Explosions Poster: www.osha.gov/Publications/combustibledustposter.pdf
- Hazard Communication Guidance for Combustible Dusts: www.osha.gov/Publications/3371combustible-dust.html

NIOSH

- www.cdc.gov/niosh/fire
- Firefighter fatality reports, safety advisories, and other guidance materials

NATIONAL FIRE ACADEMY

- Research Project: Developing Criteria for Proper Handling of Wood Dust Fires. www.usfa.fema.gov/pdf/efop/efo21877.pdf

NATIONAL FIRE PROTECTION ASSOCIATION (NFPA)

- NFPA Standard 1620, "Pre-Incident Planning"
- Several combustible dust-related standards, including 61, 484, 644, 654, and 655
- Fire Inspection Manual
- Fire Protection Handbook
- Fire Protection Guide to Hazardous Materials

INTERNATIONAL CODE COUNCIL'S INTERNATIONAL FIRE CODE

- Chapter 22, Combustible Dust Producing Operations
- Section 406, Employee Training and Response Procedures
- Section 407, Hazard Communication
- Table 5003.1.1(1), Maximum allowable quantities and requirements specific to combustible dust

NATIONAL OCEANIC AND ATMOSPHERIC ADMINISTRATION

- Chemical Reactivity Worksheet

FM GLOBAL

- Data Sheet 10-2, "Emergency Response"
- Data Sheet 7-73, "Dust Collectors and Collection Systems"
- Data Sheet 7-76, "Prevention and Mitigation of Combustible Dust Explosion and Fire"

Appendix A—Dust Collection Equipment

Dust collectors, also referred to as air-material separators, are a type of equipment commonly used in industry to remove particles from dust-laden air streams. Dust collectors are also the industrial equipment in which combustible dust explosions most frequently occur in the United States. This is because of their commonplace use and because dust collectors capture and store fine dust particles, which tend to be extremely combustible.

There are many different types of dust collectors, including cyclones, baghouses and water wash systems. This appendix describes how these operations differ, but all systems collect potentially combustible dusts and such systems should be approached with caution. All three types of dust collectors come in many different shapes and sizes—from large baghouses found in multi-story structures to small cyclones the size of a standard refrigerator. Most dust collectors are typically found outside facility structures (e.g., along building perimeters, on top of large buildings), but some facilities operate dust collectors inside buildings. The size and placement of these systems will determine, and sometimes limit, means for external access and egress. Large systems atop buildings, for example, might be accessible only by ladder. Typically, all or part of dust collectors will be permit-required confined spaces (29 CFR 1910.146).

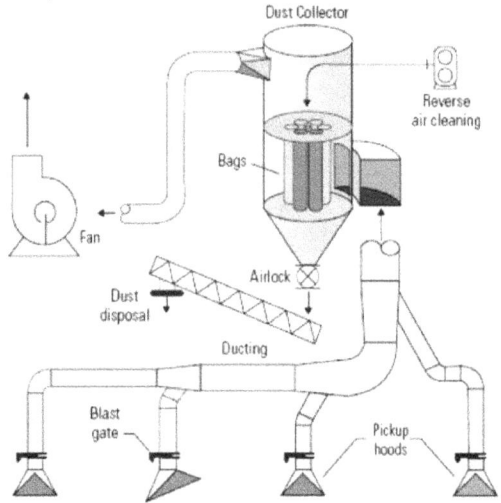

Figure 1. Dust collection system diagram

Cyclone

The dust-conveying air stream enters the cyclone unit and is sent into a circular motion, forcing the dust particles, especially the larger ones, to the inside perimeter of the unit. The particles then settle down the sides and collect at the bottom. The conveying air is discharged through baffles near the top or is ducted to a baghouse. The air is either sent for further processing or discharged from the building; it is unusual that air from a cyclone is returned to the building. Note whether the equipment is inside or outside the building.

Figure 2. Cyclone dust collector

The cone at the bottom of a cyclone will collect the dust—and it would fill up without a way to remove the dust. Since air discharging through the bottom of the cone would make it inoperable, the collected dust is usually discharged through some type of airlock valve to prevent the loss of air and dispersion of the material. Once the dust passes through the valve, it can be collected in a closed or open container under the cyclone or moved mechanically or pneumatically to a remote location.

Responders should always assume that a dangerous amount of dust is present in the bottom of a cyclone's cone. Similarly, the parts of the cyclone above the cone will have a film of dust, and access methods must consider the need to avoid suspending the dust and preventing its ignition.

Cyclones are often constructed with explosion relief panels and access doors that can be opened without cutting tools. The opening will allow air into the cyclone, however, which can intensify an internal fire or even create an internal explosion. Suppression operations should avoid the front of the cyclone's principal material openings (inlets and discharges) and the hinged sides of doors/panels. Responders should always approach a cyclone knowing that there is the potential for an internal explosion at any time. This caution is relevant even if the explosion panels are opened before emergency personnel arrive, as secondary explosions are possible.

Baghouse

Dust-conveying air streams typically enter the top of a baghouse and then pass through groups of side-by-side bags that form a filter. Once the air passes through the bag filters, it is considered to be on the clean side of the baghouse. The dirty side is usually considered to be the lower part of the enclosure, which usually has sloped collection cones or pyramids to hold the dust as it falls out of the airstream and/or off the bags. The bags are held in metal frames suspended from a metal plate, often called a tube sheet. The bags and the metal plate form a physical separation between the dirty and clean sides. Generally, baghouses can collect smaller dust particles than other methods, because the bags forming the filter bank can be chosen to capture a particular size dust.

Figure 3. *Dry baghouse*

The bags themselves can be made of a variety of materials, including cotton, combustible synthetics and fire-resistant synthetics such as Nomex® and PBI Kevlar. To maintain operations and the efficiency of the baghouse, a control unit regularly activates a cleaning cycle through all of the bags. The cleaning action could be a pulse of high-pressure air or a mechanical stroking of the bags. The collected "dust clumps" on the bags are loosened by the action of the air or stroking and fall to the bottom of the collector.

Because the bags are more efficient than cyclones at dust collection, a dangerous amount of dust is unlikely to build up in the clean side. Therefore, the air stream from the clean side of the baghouse may be discharged outside the building or, possibly, returned inside. NFPA standards and local codes address air recirculation. Note whether the equipment is inside or outside the building.

Like cyclones, baghouses have several access doors on both the clean and dirty sides of the collector. Explosion relief panels may also be found on the dirty side, where the dust is contained. As with cyclones, a potentially dangerous amount of dust will likely be present within the collector, particularly on the dirty side below the tube sheet and bags.

Responders should always approach a baghouse assuming that there could be an internal explosion at any time. This is true even if the explosion panels are already opened before emergency personnel arrive, as secondary explosions are possible, particularly when the bag-cleaning cycle is activated. Emergency responders should not stand directly in the path of either doors or explosion relief panels. Access, especially to the lower portions of the baghouse, could result in a dust cloud explosion hazard when collected material is disturbed or metal-on-metal contact generates a spark. Emergency responders should seriously consider whether it is urgent to access or fight fires in a dust baghouse, as either activity could result in a dust explosion. It may be better to use a defensive attack mode and monitor the situation.

It is also important for responders to realize that when power to a dust collection system is shut down, the dust collected on the exterior of the bags within the baghouse often falls off once the air flow across the bag surfaces has stopped. This could easily create an explosible dust cloud inside the baghouse on the dirty side. Therefore, emergency responders need to coordinate with facility personnel before shutting off the power to a dust collection system and exercise extreme caution when doing so.

Water Wash

Water wash is a style of dust collection involving the air stream passing through a water spray or wall of water film that collects the dust. The water is usually recirculated and could have chemicals added to control foaming or other performance-diminishing characteristics. The dust settles out in a sump and the water may pass through filters to remove finer dust. Water wash is most often used to collect metal dust. It is also sometimes used for material, such as coal, that tends to leave a residue when dried.

These systems have a water sump that should be checked for flammable gas during emergency operations near the sump. When dry, the once-wet areas will usually have a covering of fine metal powder on vertical surfaces and potentially thicker amounts on horizontal surfaces. Avoid actions that may disturb the dust or suspend it in air.

Appendix B—Storage Methods

Silo

A silo is a tall, slender cylinder-shaped structure rather than a tank, hopper, or bin. A silo can be a single unit or arranged into interconnected groups of silos. When four silos are arranged in a group, the star-shaped space between them can also be used for storage.

Silos are filled from the top. Dust clouds are often generated during filling and can fill most of the ullage (unfilled) spaces. When filling ceases, the dust clouds typically settle onto the stored materials.

Figure 1. *Bucket elevator and storage silo*

Silos are emptied from the bottom, typically through control valves (with gravity as the only force moving material out of the silo). The material is often deposited on moving belts and carried to elevators to raise it to higher levels for processing or movement to trucks, rail cars, barges, or ships. Some silos are elevated themselves, so that trucks can drive under them to receive material. The discharge process usually generates dust, with the volume depending on the distance the material falls and the rate at which it moves. Tunnels under silos need frequent cleaning to remove the dust and material that falls from the conveyor system. The bearings in conveying systems have been the ignition source for many dust explosions in the past. Regular inspection and lubrication are key to preventing overheating and operational failure.

Newer silos are typically constructed of metal, glass-coated or enameled metal, or concrete. Many older silos, however, are constructed of various types of tile and brick. For each construction material, there are unique challenges regarding the methods needed to breach the silo wall. Cutting metal walls, for example, often involves methods that generate sparks or heat—both possible ignition sources.

Material movement through a silo is uncontrolled; this means that for some materials, gaps can form during filling and dispensing. In addition, some products may not support the weight of a person standing on them in a silo. For both reasons, a responder could become engulfed in the material, which is an extremely hazardous and life-threatening situation. Lifelines, harnesses and boards to spread out a person's weight need to be available should an emergency responder need to enter a silo.

Hopper/Bin

A hopper, or bin, is a smaller storage unit that is often connected or used with a specific machine or group of production machines. It may contain raw material, finished product, or waste from the production. The actual contents will determine the hazard and the means of response.

A person generally would not be expected to enter this type of storage container. When hoppers and bins are part of the production equipment, product fires can spread into them from a production malfunction. Hoppers and bins can be elevated on legs, supported by the equipment, or rest on the floor; the pre-incident survey should include procedures for safely reaching these positions. As part of the survey process, the contents of hoppers and bins should be identified. For instance, it is helpful to know the type of material stored (e.g., pulverized coal, grain dust, resin dust) and the physical properties of the material (e.g., particle size distribution, moisture content). With detailed knowledge of the contents of hoppers and bins, the hazards of the contents can be determined and incorporated into the IAP.

Bunker

A bunker is a larger storage unit, typically horizontal and on the ground (or sometimes in the ground). The term can also be used for large vertical storage of raw material. In some cases, it can be difficult to access material stored inside a bunker. Bunkers sometimes involve heavy construction, and the depth or width of the stored material makes the center a long way from the perimeter or surface.

Bunkers are filled from the top, like silos, and they have the same ullage (unfilled) area dust cloud issues. Horizontal bunkers often generate less dust than vertical storage systems, given the shorter fall distance from the loading mechanism.

Tanks

Tanks typically are stationary storage containers, large enough for a person to enter, with gravity discharge. Tanks are most often used for liquid storage, but dusts and finely divided solids can also be stored in them. Responders should consider likely emergency scenarios for tanks used to store dusts and finely divided solids.

Photo: M. Chibbaro

Figure 2. Tanks

Emergency personnel should not enter tanks without following confined space safety procedures (29 CFR 1910.146). Sometimes it is best to handle a fire emergency involving a tank by closing the tank and waiting for lack of oxygen to extinguish the fire. In other words,

the risk associated with entering or accessing external tanks often exceeds the risks associated with letting a fire burn in an enclosed vessel; emergency personnel should consider taking a defensive attack mode in these cases.

Bulk Piles

Bulk piles can be located indoors or outdoors and can have open sides, partial sides to allow the pile of material to be higher with a smaller base, or no siding—simply material on a grade, allowed to take whatever shape gravity allows. In any of these configurations, extensive quantities of dust can be piled several feet deep. This is hazardous: normal operations can easily disperse the dust into the air, creating the possibility of a series of explosions. While any explosion hazard is significant, indoor pile storage can have extreme consequences. Responders should take a close look at appropriate responses to any situation involving extensive quantities of openly stored combustible dusts.

Almost any material can be stored in a bulk pile—coal, grain and wood chips, among others. The hazard will vary with the material and how it is placed into the pile. For example, flat indoor grain storage can include the full range of grain sizes, from dust to full kernels. As it is moved either into or out of storage, dust will be generated. A nearly empty storage area could have piles of dust on the floor. Facility personnel on the pre-incident survey team are encouraged to document the types of materials that are expected to be present based on their familiarity with typical plant conditions.

Piles tend to self-heat, especially outdoors. There is a science relating to compaction of coal or similar materials to allow heat dissipation while minimizing moisture and air infiltration. Smoldering piles may be spread out and wetted if doing so is possible without forming a dust cloud.

Waste Receptacles (e.g., Dumpsters, Trash Compactors)

Both dumpsters and trash compactors are examples of waste receptacles that are potential sources of dust explosions. Unless a facility has rigid guidelines and security, the range of materials in its waste and recycling containers will be extensive. Responders should view waste receptacles in facilities with combustible dusts as explosion hazards.

Unloading a dumpster containing a large amount of combustible dust clearly can be hazardous because the activity can generate a dust cloud. However, even when dumpsters are not being unloaded and dust clouds are not visible, emergency responders should assume the presence of combustible dusts when they respond to fires in dumpsters. Facility owners should try to place dumpsters where an incident will not spread to the facility or involve exterior equipment such as dust collection systems (e.g., baghouses). When dealing with a dumpster fire, emergency responders should avoid firefighting actions that could create a dust cloud. It may be prudent to assume a defensive attack mode, protecting exposures and cooling the receptacle.

Whereas dumpsters are typically detached, trash compactors are often connected directly to the facility. Trash compactors attached to a building's interior through loading doors or chutes can allow an explosion or fire to spread into the building. Any access doors between the trash compactor and the facility need to be designed to self-close and latch. The building area around the loading door or chute should be clear of accumulated dust and waste to keep explosions and fires from spreading. Emergency responders should be aware that interior access to trash compactors can be difficult—and that dust from collection systems often ends up in trash compactors. The pre-incident survey team should address the potential for dust explosions when anticipating emergency response actions involving trash compactors.

Spontaneous Ignition in Storage

It is not uncommon for coal and wood chips to self-heat and begin burning without a separate ignition source. This most often occurs in outdoor pile storage, but it is possible with other kinds of storage.

When smoldering fires occur in a pile, they can be difficult to identify and to extinguish. Many factors make spontaneous ignition hard to anticipate. For example, the potential for coal to self-heat depends on the type of coal, its size, and how the bulk pile is assembled. One of the main concerns with deep-seated fires is that emergency responder actions could generate a dust cloud that leads to an explosion.

Emergency responders should avoid using straight-stream suppression attacks, as they can cause dust clouds to form as well as kick up burning material. The pre-incident survey team should evaluate hazards involving bulk pile storage and assess the possibility of fighting deep-seated pile fires. To avoid creating explosion hazards, emergency responders should be aware of bulk pile dust hazards.

Emergency responders should also avoid walking or driving onto burning piles. Fires can burn out a core area — in which case the pile may appear solid on top, but is unable to support the load of a person or vehicle. A collapse will drop whatever is on top into a burning hole that can then flare up from the sudden introduction of air.

Appendix C—Process Equipment

Dryers and Ovens

Dryers and ovens are used to dry or heat materials as part of a process. They can be classified into two operational groups: continuous and batch.

Figure 1. *Ring dryer*

Batch dryers and ovens are typically loaded, operated and then unloaded. Dust is generally produced only during loading and unloading. Sometimes, however, the internal ventilation used to increase drying or heating performance can dislodge dusts and small particles, which then settle within the dryer or oven.

In a continuous dryer or oven, material is carried through the space (by conveyor belts, mobile carts, cranes, etc.), and can be dislodged or produce dust that settles on interior surfaces. Deposited material can remain, start a fire, or help one to spread. When attending to an incident in a dryer or oven, responders are likely to find combustibles throughout the equipment. Drying or heating can generate combustible dusts if the original material was in solution. In an emergency involving dryers and ovens, responders need to take great care to systematically eliminate the potential hazards. Explosions have occurred during operations as well as during facility investigations, when the unit has stopped working and personnel are trying to identify the source of failure.

Responders may encounter dryers inside or outside, even in areas where codes or standards require or recommend that they be outside. Responders need to be aware of all such equipment, regardless of its location.

The first step in most situations is to shut down the heating systems, which are often the ignition sources of most immediate concern. Ventilation systems should stay running to prevent the accumulation of potentially explosible vapors or combustion gases (i.e., unburned gases emitted during incomplete combustion).

For continuous dryers and ovens, the equipment feeding material should be shut off. Removal of material already inside depends on whether it is involved in a fire and if continued exposure to heat as the oven cools presents a more significant risk. Continuous dryers may also have an abort gate that redirects burning material to a safe location. The pre-incident survey team should discuss these issues and establish a strategy that limits the risk of fire or explosion associated with shutting down the process material flow. Responders must also recognize any hazards involving the contents, gaseous by-products, or combustion products that might be generated as part of the drying process.

Spray Drying Equipment

As spray drying equipment has become more popular, fire experience has prompted many significant improvements to the equipment operation and controls. In a spray dryer, large volumes of heated air rapidly remove moisture from liquids or semisolids by spraying/atomizing the material to be dried in the air stream. The resulting solids are removed by cyclones and dust collection equipment. Milk and eggs are examples of common food products that are spray-dried.

Dust and finely divided combustible solids are part of the finished product. When air circulation is interrupted, these solids fall and collect at the bottom of the unit. Heat is used to remove moisture; this heating is known to cause smoldering fires and restarting the air circulation has caused explosions from the smoldering fires. Explosions have also occurred when equipment was opened to extinguish the internal fires.

Internal hot spots can be identified from the outside using thermal imaging cameras and temperature measurements of exterior walls. Removing the heat is one way to reduce ignition sources. However, introducing water could cause a dryer to collapse from the weight of the water. Responders should determine whether water-based suppression agents are appropriate to use inside a dryer and, if so, calculate the maximum amount of suppression agent to be used. (Dried-product collection equipment should be treated the same as the dust collection equipment described in this appendix, in terms of potential dust explosion hazards.)

Size-Reduction Operations

Many materials must be reduced in size during processing operations. Equipment such as grinders, pulverizers and hammer mills are used for size reduction. When most materials are reduced in size, dust and solid fines are generated. The process of size reduction also generates heat, as well as metal (often called tramp metal) that breaks off inside the equipment. Both can be ignition sources for fires and explosions. To reduce this risk, facilities can take steps - such as dust control and removal, use of magnets to catch tramp metal and equipment cooling.

Emergency response must include positive lockout of power supplies (electrical and/or mechanical) and the blocking or securing of rotating elements to prevent movement. The material (e.g., chains, cables, wedges, wood blocks) and methods to accomplish the blocking or securing should be part of the plan. Responders should approach size reduction equipment as they would other dust-containing enclosed equipment to avoid dispersing the contents into the air. Incidents that occur while the machine is operating will involve materials inside the enclosure in a range of sizes, including fine dust. The potential for an explosion is increased by the amount of fine dust generated by the process. The particle size of the finished product should be noted.

Pre-incident survey activities should include a review of facility safety and suppression systems. This allows the team to understand when and under what circumstances such resources will be used or activated. In some cases, there may be automatic activation. Size reduction processes can have extensive fugitive dust issues if there is no dust collection system or if the dust collection system is poorly designed. Facility personnel on the pre-incident survey team should accurately portray typical conditions so that the team can assess the dust explosion hazard in the facility and near the size-reduction processing equipment.

Appendix D—Pneumatic Conveying Equipment

Industrial manufacturing facilities use many methods to move bulk solid materials through their production processes—for example, belt conveyors, screw conveyors and bucket elevators. Certain facilities use pneumatic conveyors to transfer materials; these are completely enclosed tubing, piping, or ductwork that can transport solids both vertically and horizontally. Pneumatic conveying systems can transport a wide range of materials, including process feedstock, finished products and even wastes collected in production areas.

Figure 1. Conveying system piping

Pneumatic conveying systems function by gases—most commonly air—carried through the tubing or ductwork at velocities high enough to push the solid material from one unit operation to the next. Pneumatic conveyance systems can operate under either positive or negative pressure. Positive pressure systems use blowers that push materials through piping or ductwork, whereas negative pressure systems use vacuum equipment to move material.

Pneumatic conveying systems are not ideal for transporting all materials, particularly solids with large particle size or high bulk density. There are two main pneumatic conveyance types: dilute phase and dense phase. (Both methods can be used with either positive or negative pressure.) Dilute phase conveyance is the most common method for transporting materials and is better suited for powders or granules with light bulk densities. In this case, the systems operate at low pressure and high velocities, which helps keep particles in suspension. Dense phase conveyance involves transferring materials at low velocities and high pressures without suspending particles.

Explosions in pneumatic conveying systems occur because they often are used to transport heated and dried particles between process components that are potential ignition sources, such as hammer mills, ovens and direct-fired dryers. Factors leading to explosions may include: (1) static electricity generated when particles contact other particles or contact the walls of pneumatic conveying systems; (2) heated or smoldering material transported from grinding or drying processes into the pneumatic conveying systems; (3) frictional heating caused by tramp metal that inadvertently enters the systems; and (4) charged powder emitted to the atmosphere, which combines with electrostatic sparks.

Pneumatic conveying systems typically have safety controls to mitigate the effects of fires and explosions. Examples of these controls include venting, suppression and pressure containment. Spark detection and extinguishing systems can also be useful in pneumatic conveying systems because they are designed to extinguish sparks or embers as soon as they are detected. These controls can also be interlocked with abort gates, alarms and other measures designed to prevent hazards and alert facility personnel of unsafe conditions. A fire detection system should also include an interlocking device that will automatically shut down any devices that feed materials into the pneumatic conveyance system as soon as fire is detected. Other controls may also be used to ensure safe operation of these systems, such as flooding with inert gases and pressure containment.

Emergency responders should be careful when fighting fires near pneumatic conveying systems for several reasons:

■ Because the systems are essentially pressurized streams of air, any breach or failure in the pipes, tubes, or ducts in a positive pressure operational pneumatic conveying system can release large quantities of combustible dust into the air. Therefore, should an incident breach a pneumatic conveying system—or should firefighting activities cause such a breach—an explosible dust cloud could be created quickly in areas where firefighters are working.

■ Even if a facility confirms that a pneumatic conveying system is no longer transporting solids, the system can still present a hazard. Breaches in pneumatic conveying systems can worsen existing hazards by increasing the amount of air available to a fire or possibly dispersing dust that had settled outside the ductwork. This concern is greatest for positive pressure systems but can also be a hazard in negative pressure systems, depending on the location of the breach.

■ A possible question during some firefighting incidents is whether facilities should shut down their pneumatic conveying systems. Some facilities will have automatic interlocks that trigger purging and other shutdown mechanisms. If they do not or if these interlocks fail, responders should evaluate the trade-offs between shutting down the system (which would halt the air flow but leave tubes, pipes, or ducts potentially full of combustible dusts) or purging the system (which would remove the potentially explosible material but could also cause smoldering material to travel through the system, depending on the specifics of the incident). It is best to work with facility personnel on these matters.

Emergency responders should be aware of these possibilities in case this type of failure occurs during the initial incident and the pneumatic conveyance system is still operational.

OSHA Regional Offices

Region I
Boston Regional Office
(CT*, ME, MA, NH, RI, VT*)
JFK Federal Building, Room E340
Boston, MA 02203
(617) 565-9860 (617) 565-9827 Fax

Region II
New York Regional Office
(NJ*, NY*, PR*, VI*)
201 Varick Street, Room 670
New York, NY 10014
(212) 337-2378 (212) 337-2371 Fax

Region III
Philadelphia Regional Office
(DE, DC, MD*, PA, VA*, WV)
The Curtis Center
170 S. Independence Mall West
Suite 740 West
Philadelphia, PA 19106-3309
(215) 861-4900 (215) 861-4904 Fax

Region IV
Atlanta Regional Office
(AL, FL, GA, KY*, MS, NC*, SC*, TN*)
61 Forsyth Street, SW, Room 6T50
Atlanta, GA 30303
(678) 237-0400 (678) 237-0447 Fax

Region V
Chicago Regional Office
(IL*, IN*, MI*, MN*, OH, WI)
230 South Dearborn Street
Room 3244
Chicago, IL 60604
(312) 353-2220 (312) 353-7774 Fax

Region VI
Dallas Regional Office
(AR, LA, NM*, OK, TX)
525 Griffin Street, Room 602
Dallas, TX 75202
(972) 850-4145 (972) 850-4149 Fax
(972) 850-4150 FSO Fax

Region VII
Kansas City Regional Office
(IA*, KS, MO, NE)
Two Pershing Square Building
2300 Main Street, Suite 1010
Kansas City, MO 64108-2416
(816) 283-8745 (816) 283-0547 Fax

Region VIII
Denver Regional Office
(CO, MT, ND, SD, UT*, WY*)
Cesar Chavez Memorial Building
1244 Speer Boulevard, Suite 551
Denver, CO 80204
(720) 264-6550 (720) 264-6585 Fax

Region IX
San Francisco Regional Office
(AZ*, CA*, HI*, NV*, and American Samoa,
Guam and the Northern Mariana Islands)
90 7th Street, Suite 18100
San Francisco, CA 94103
(415) 625-2547 (415) 625-2534 Fax

Region X
Seattle Regional Office
(AK*, ID, OR*, WA*)
300 Fifth Avenue, Suite 1280
Seattle, WA 98104
(206) 757-6700 (206) 757-6705 Fax

* These states and territories operate their own OSHA-approved job safety and health plans and cover state and local government employees as well as private sector employees. The Connecticut, Illinois, New Jersey, New York and Virgin Islands programs cover public employees only. (Private sector workers in these states are covered by Federal OSHA). States with approved programs must have standards that are identical to, or at least as effective as, the Federal OSHA standards.

Note: To get contact information for OSHA area offices, OSHA-approved state plans and OSHA consultation projects, please visit us online at www.osha.gov or call us at 1-800-321-OSHA (6742).

How to Contact OSHA

For questions or to get information or advice,
to report an emergency, report a fatality or
catastrophe, order publications, sign up for
OSHA's e-newsletter *QuickTakes*, or to file a
confidential complaint, contact your nearest
OSHA office, visit www.osha.gov or call OSHA
at 1-800-321-OSHA (6742), TTY 1-877-889-5627.

**For assistance, contact us.
We are OSHA. We can help.**